Fashion Bead Embroidery

Fashion Bead Embroidery

Natalie Giltsoff

B. T. Batsford Limited   London
Charles T. Branford Company   Newton   Massachusetts

TO THOSE WHO TAUGHT ME

First published 1971
7134 2646 2

Branford SBN 8231 4025 3
Library of Congress Catalog Card Number 79 131434

Filmset in 11 on 12-pt Bembo by
Keyspools Ltd, Golborne, Lancashire
Printed and bound in Denmark by
F. E. Bording Limited, Copenhagen
for the publishers
B. T. Batsford Limited
4 Fitzhardinge Street, London W1 and
Charles T. Branford Company
28 Union Street, Newton Centre, Massachusetts 02159

Contents

Acknowledgment

Beads and sequins are some of the most difficult things to photograph well. I am therefore most grateful to Derek Mossman who took so expertly the majority of photographs for this book.

I should also like to thank Jane Hood who was responsible for the fashion drawings, figures 18 to 21, and Constance Howard who lent many interesting pieces of bead work from her personal collection, figures 2, 5, 9, 26, 38, 39, 41 and 44.

I am, too, indebted to the staffs and students of the following schools and colleges, without whose co-operation I could never have gathered such a wide range of work:

Past and present students at Wall Hall College, Aldenham, Watford, Hertfordshire, for figures 22, 24 and 25; First, Second and Third year students at The College of Fashion and Clothing Technology, London W1 for figures 1, 8, 17, 28, 29, 30, 40, 50 and 55; London College of Furniture, London N1 for figure 10; Ealing Technical College and School of Art, Fashion Department, London W6 for figures 23 and 32; Hornsey College of Art, Fashion Department, London N15 for figures 6, 43, 46 and 53; and Second and Third year students from the Embroidery and Fashion Departments at Manchester Polytechnic for figures 11, 16 and 36.

I should like to thank Terry Waddington, for taking the photographs of students' work at Manchester Polytechnic.

Last, but not least, I wish to thank all my long-suffering friends, who helped, encouraged, advised and tolerated me while I was working on this book, for I thought and talked of nothing else but beads, beads and more beads.

N G

Camberwell, London, 1971

Introduction

From the earliest times, beading has been used as a form of decoration; both the primitive and more advanced civilisations found an excuse (if excuse was needed) to adorn themselves, or their possessions, with a richer surface than the original. In Europe, particularly during the nineteenth century, there was an upsurge of the craft, when all manner of things were given the added embellishment of bead work.

As bead embroidery is an expensive craft, serving no purpose other than decoration, we are rather more selective with our embellishments today. The aim of this book is to help to re-create, in a new way, the ancient art of 'surface enrichment'.

There are many ways in which beads and sequins can be used but here I am concerned mainly with hand-sewn bead embroidery on dress and accessories.

If time is to be spent doing good and exciting work it is always wothwhile to use the best materials. These need not necessarily be the most expensive. Man-made fibres have reached an unprecedented level, and are no longer regarded as substitutes for natural fibres.

As dress embroidery is very much linked to fashion, and subject to frequent change, I make no attempt to suggest the style of garment to be used, neither do I discuss the current trends in fashion. I would, however, stress that bead embroidery should enhance both the design and appearance of the garment, giving it an exclusive quality.

Materials

It is because the sewing thread between each bead must have an even tension if the beads are to lie correctly on the surface of the fabric, that bead embroidery is best worked on a rectangular frame. This frame should always be large enough to take the whole piece of work, for it is essential to see at a glance what has been accomplished. In this way the embroidery will be kept fresh and lively, and no area will be over- or under-worked, also the balance of the design, its colour and emphasis can be continually revised.

Generally, bead work requires a backing material such as lawn, muslin, mull calico or even a fine woollen interfacing (the type of backing is determined by the working material). The backing fabric, which must be stretched evenly, though allowing a little give over the frame, serves two essential purposes. Firstly, it is a foundation onto which the working fabric can be stretched without distorting the grain of the fabric. Secondly, it gives the material an extra firmness that helps to take the weight of thickly sewn beads, thus helping to prevent the beads from pulling or puckering the work. The exceptions to this rule are sheer fabrics, such as chiffon, net and organdie, machine and hand knitted fabrics, or an article on which separately beaded motifs are applied. Pale colours such as white, pale yellow and lilac are easily rubbed during working, so it is advisable to tack sheets of clean white tissue paper round the outer edges of the work, using stabbing stitches and a machine embroidery thread. Apart from doing this, when not working on the embroidery, wrap it and the frame in a clean white cloth.

Before setting up embroidery frames (this is known as *dressing a frame*) find and mark the centres on all four sides of the frame, the backing material, and the working fabric. It is from these marks that the backing is attached to the frame, and the working fabric to the backing. The main reason for this is to ensure an even distribution of tension and the correct alignment of the warp and weft threads. Remove selvedges from all materials and always cut them to a thread. Place the fabrics onto the frame with the warp and weft threads running vertically and horizontally to it.

The frame should always be held between two supports of a similar height, this then leaves both hands free to manipulate the work. It could be supported between two chair backs or two tables, but for refinement, between two trestles with adjustable arm pieces, so that the work can be at any height.

Dressing a frame

Slate frame   On this type of frame the backing material is sewn on two sides to a tape or webbing with over-cast stitches, using a strong linen or button thread. Start at the centre marks each time and stitch towards the end of the tape. The other two sides of the fabric are fixed to the frame with a strong string which is laced through the sides of the backing and over the wood. These loops should not be more than 50 mm (2 in.) apart. Wind the ends of the string around the frame and tie off. A packing needle is usually used for the string. See diagram 1A.

Making a frame

If the piece of work is too large to fit onto a slate frame, then a simple method of construction for making one to take the work is to use halp lap joints as indicated in diagram 2B. These joints are satisfactory as well as being relatively easy to construct.

Though large stretchers may seem rather cumbersome, they are in fact not as difficult to use as may at first appear. All the sections of the pattern for the jacket (see colour plate facing page 60) were worked on a frame 1220×915 mm (4×3 ft).

Use 25×50 mm (1×2 in.) wood (these measurements are approximate as wood sizes vary). Take four pieces of wood cut to the required lengths. Now cut two sections 50×12 mm (2×½ in.) out of each piece, thus making eight cuts in all. Diagrams 2A and 2B.

Interlock the four pieces of wood as shown in diagram 2C, and check that the four corners are at right angles to each other. This is done by taking a piece of string, or straight edge and placing it on one of the corners. Measure the length of the diagonal between two corners. Place this measurement on the second diagonal, and when both diagonals tally exactly all four corners will be at right angles. Fix together with a strong wood glue and a few panel pins or screws. Diagram 2D.

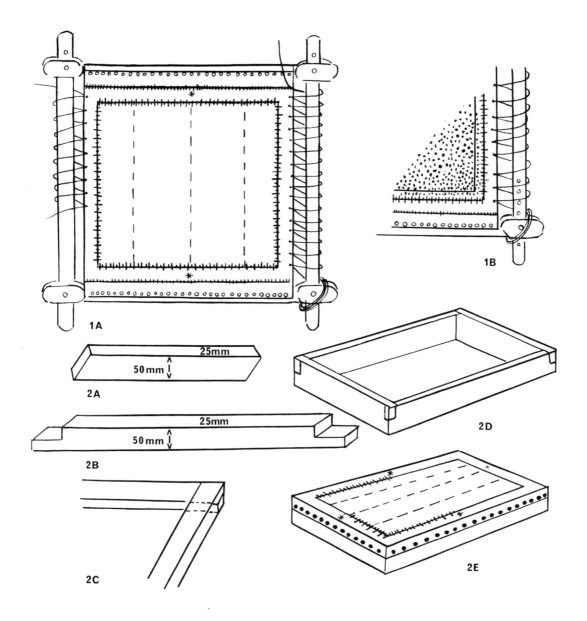

1A

1B

2A

25mm

50mm

2B

25mm

50mm

2C

2D

2E

Then with medium coarse and fine sand paper, gently file the sharp edges of the wood down so that they become slightly rounded. If this is not done, the sharp edges could tear or permanently mark the materials.

To attach the backing material to this type of frame, use gold headed drawing pins or staples, placing them at intervals of about 6 mm ($\frac{1}{4}$ in.) apart. Make sure that they are pushed well into the wood, and that the material is straight and taut as in diagram 2E.

Fix the working fabric onto the backing, as described below.

Artists' canvas stretchers

Canvas stretchers, which come in a variety of sizes can also be used for embroidery. They are bought from most good art shops, but they may be rather expensive. Old picture frames can be adapted and used as stretchers though on the whole these are heavy and cumbersome. Stretch fabrics onto either type of frame,

Removing backing fabric from stretched materials

Cover the frame with a backing material as described on page 10. Fix the working material to this with long and short stitches, use either a silk thread, machine embroidery thread, or even a fine wool, depending on the type of fabric to be used. After both the fabrics have been fixed to the frame, remove the three lines of tacking stitches and carefully cut the backing material away from the back of the working fabric. The working fabric is thus stretched to the frame but is free from backing material, except around the outer edges and this is removed once the work is complete (diagram 1B). When beading on transparent fabrics start and finish off the thread between each bead or group of beads. If this is not done the embroidery could be spoilt by the thread showing through on the right side of the work.

Attaching the working fabric

The backing fabric should be at least 50 mm (2 in.) larger than the working fabric (diagram 2E). Never cut the garment or piece out to size, but leave a similar 50 mm (2 in.) margin plus seam allowance and turnings. The backing, as already mentioned takes the stresses and strains of being stretched tightly over the frame, and so too does the extra material around the piece of bead work. Should the embroidery need to be stretched or shrunk the extra material will also allow for this. Avoid pulling or stretching the working material, but gently ease it into place, keeping the edges as straight as possible. Fix to the backing using long and short stitches (diagram 1A). These should fall on different threads of the fabric to ensure an even measure of tension. Always sew from the centre marks to the left, or to the right. A machine embroidery thread matching the colour of the working fabric is probably the best thread to use, since it is fine and will leave little or no marks in the work. Sewing cottons tend to leave small holes or tiny pieces of fluff in the embroidery; these get caught in between the warp and weft threads of the materials, and they are never satisfactorily removed. After attaching one side of the working fabric to the backing tack three lines. One up the centre of the frame and two either side of it. (See diagram 1A.) This keeps both the materials together while stitching the other three sides.

Transferring designs

Apart from transferring designs by free hand, there are also several other methods of doing this, a few of which are described below. For tacking out designs it is advisable to use a machine embroidery thread of the same colour as the base fabric and not a contrasting colour. This thread is often left in the work as it sometimes becomes firmly sewn in with the beads and if it were in a contrasting colour it would obviously be too conspicuous. Never try to pull rows of stitching out, for this could tear the material and permanently mark it. So when removing stitches cut each stitch separately and lift off the pieces of thread.

Templates

This method is suitable for designs which are made up of large areas of beads. The paper templates are tacked onto the working material, and small stabbing stitches are worked adjacent to the outer edges of them. Once this has been done remove the templates.

Tacked tissue or tracing paper

Trace the design onto either tracing or tissue paper, using a hard pencil (2H) or a felt tipped pen, and tack the paper in the correct position onto the working material. Now tack along the pencil lines using small stabbing stitches. To remove the paper perforate it with a needle, between and under each stitch. By doing this the paper can be removed without damaging the stitches.

Transferring designs onto sheer fabrics

When working on sheer fabrics such as chiffon, net, organdie and silks etc, outline the design onto paper, using a hard pencil or a felt tipped pen. Place the paper underneath the material and securely pin into position. As sheer fabrics are easily damaged do not sew them to the paper design, but with small running stitches follow the lines of the design. By doing this the paper can be easily removed without damage to the material.

Pricking and pouncing

Pricking and pouncing which has its origins in early Renaissance frescoes, is a method by which a design can be readily transferred and repeated. This method is only important if the design is of a complex nature, which needs to be repeated more than two or three times.

Method Draw the design onto tracing paper and with a sharp needle fixed to a piece of wood, or special pricker, perforate the paper along the lines of the design. The paper should always be pricked over a thick soft surface, for example a blanket. With gold headed drawing pins secure the working fabric to a wooden surface. On top of this place the pricked design, also firmly fixed with drawing pins. Use either pouncing powder or powdered charcoal, mixed with a little white chalk on pale colours, and powdered white chalk on dark colours. With a small round pad, dab the powder over the tracing paper. Finally finish off this process by gently rubbing all over the surface of the paper so that the powder is forced through the tiny holes onto the material. Fix the design by painting over the dots with a water colour paint. If this is not done the design will be rubbed away once the fabric is moved. It is because the design is permanently painted onto the material that this method is unsuitable for free adaptions of the original design. Fix to the backing fabric in the usual way.

Stretching bead work

Once removed from its frame a finished piece of bead work may pucker and lose its shape. If this does happen stretch the embroidery over damp white blotting paper. This method shrinks the areas that have become stretched and puckered, and stretches those areas that have become too tightly sewn.

Place two or three layers of damp blotting paper on a drawing board, or another suitable wooden surface. This should be larger than the piece of work. Lay the bead work on top of the paper with the beaded side facing upwards. If the embroidery has sequins worked on it take extra care, for sequins are inclined to curl and melt when they come in contact with water. To prevent this from happening, only damp the first layer of paper, and place another layer of dry paper on top of it. Use gold headed drawing pins for pinning out the work, as these do not rust so easily.

Beading thread

Make sure that at least one edge of the work is straight and secure it with the drawing pins, set 50 mm (2 in.) apart. Work around the embroidery placing the pins at an equal distance, at the same time ease it into shape. Continue putting in the pins until they are touching one another. For really large pieces 4 to 6 boxes of pins may be required. Leave the work to dry for at least twenty-four hours. Cottons, silks and wool threads should always be coated with a little bees-wax, as this gives extra strength. Pull the thread through the wax several times, and then evenly distribute the wax along the thread by pulling it through the thumb and index finger. Waxing also helps the beads to slide more easily along the thread as well as preventing them from rubbing their way through it too quickly. Sewing cottons, silks, as well as some of the newer synthetic threads are suitable for sewing on most beads, but the type of thread to be used is governed by the working material. It is obviously advisable to use a thread which matches either the colour of the beads, or the ground material. However, subtle effects can be achieved when different coloured threads are used for sewing on transparent beads. This alters their appearance and

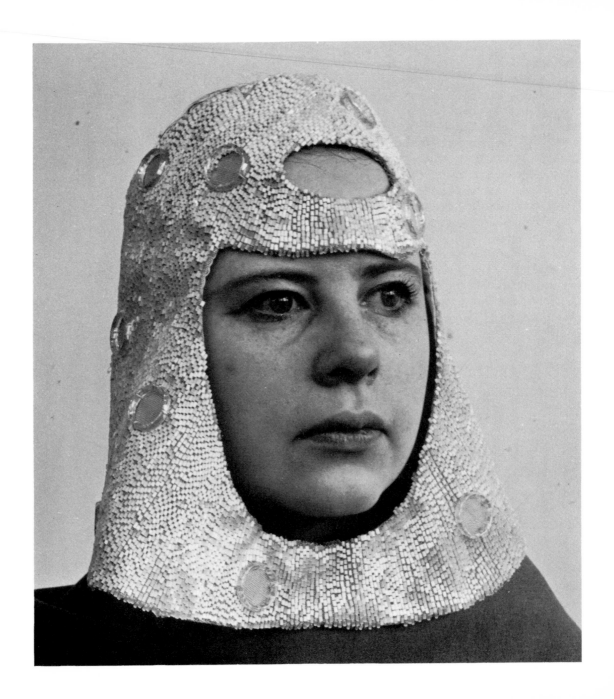

gives the work a shaded quality, though the beads may in fact be one colour and tone. (See figure 1.) The traditional concept that threads should not be knotted has no essential place in modern embroidery. The back of the work should always be as neat as possible, but this can still be achieved with knotted threads. It may also be an advantage if the thread ends are left hanging down underneath the work until the embroidery is complete. Too much insistence on finishing off each thread end, could dampen enthusiasm and inhibit a change of mind over the choice of beads, as well as the design. However, once the design is complete, properly finish off each thread by working several stitches over one another.

Some people recommend that all thread ends be held in place with a little rubber-based fabric glue, as this prevents large numbers of beads from falling off the embroidery should any of the threads get broken. Most fabric glues are washable, but their cleaning potential is rarely mentioned, neither are their solvents. Therefore, to avoid disastrous things happening to the work, it is advisable to use glue only on articles that are unlikely to be sent to dry cleaners.

Beading needles

These have elongated eyes which allow the passage of a thicker thread, although the actual needle is finer and longer than most other types. They can usually be bought from the same shops that sell beads, and they come in sizes from 12 to 18.

Sewing beads and sequins

Before sewing on the beads or sequins, make sure that the grain of the working material is straight, and that the frame has an even tension across it. Also that the main lines of the design are clearly marked on the working fabric.

It is advisable not to have the sewing thread too long as beads and sequins are sewn to the fabric by means of stabbing stitches, which are worked from the back of the embroidery to the right side of the work.

1   *Helmet designed by Reed Crawford and embroidered by first year student at The College of Fashion and Clothing Technology*

Method Start by making a small knot at one end of the thread, or work several small stiches on top of one another at the back of the work. Pass the needle through to the right side of the embroidery and pick up a bead or sequin. Slide this down the sewing thread until it is touching the working fabric. Hold the bead in place with the left hand, and with the right hand replace the needle into the fabric, to the width or height of the bead. See diagrams 3A, B and C.

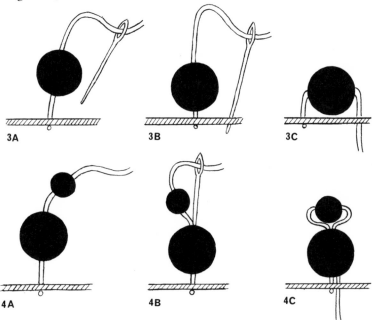

3A   3B   3C

4A   4B   4C

Diagrams 4A, B and C show how two or more beads or sequins are sewn one on top of the other. When beads or sequins are attached to the fabric in this way, they give the embroidery a rich texture as well as a high relief quality.

Beads and sequins

Beads and sequins can be bought from most good haberdashery departments, or needle-craft shops. When purchasing always bear in mind that even small pieces of work require many beads, and do check that there will be some continuity of stock.

Fabric

Following are some useful hints to bear in mind when working on various fabrics. It is advisable to wash the hands often when working for long periods, as warm hands can permanently mark fabrics.

Net

When beading on net select beads that are large enough to sit on the surface of the material, or the effect will be spoilt. When working on this delicate fabric take care not to tear it, and it is worth remembering that if the thread is not finished off between each bead, or groups of beads, the work will be spoilt by the thread showing through on the right side of the embroidery. (See figures 2 and 41.)

Woolen fabrics

The weight of the beads must be consistent with the weight of the material, i.e. the beads must not be too heavy or too small. When beading on loosely woven or textured fabrics like bouclé select beads that will not be lost in the texture. Since wool has a certain amount of elasticity it may be advisable to use a fine woollen interfacing as a backing fabric. Natural fabrics are generally at their best when they are used together.

Velvets

Silk and cotton velvets are easily marked, so mistakes must be avoided. Try not to handle them too much as warm hands can also damage the pile. If pinning the fabric always pin well within the seam allowance. Use a silk thread for attaching it to the backing fabric, which could be pre-shrunk lawn, mull or silk and also for sewing on the beads.

Silks

Heavy silks, such as wild silk, could have a fine woollen interfacing as a backing material. For lighter weight silks it might be advisable to use lawn, mull or a silk fabric. Sew beads and sequins on with a silk thread.

Knitted fabrics

Hand or machine knitted fabrics may not require a backing material, in which case the method described on page 12 under 'Removing backing fabric from stretched materials' might be used. Do not stretched knitted fabrics too tightly, as they could be pulled out of shape. It may be advisable to use a fine wool for attaching them to the frame rather than a cotton or silk thread as these could damage the stitches and cause them to run. Select beads that will not pull the material too much and allow rather more material on this kind of fabric, for if shrinkage does occur it may well be more than for other types (see page 48). A silk thread should be suitable for sewing on the beads.

2 *Metal sequins and black velvet ribbon worked on tulle, c. 1880 By courtesy of Constance Howard*

Design

What is design? Basically it is the balancing of shapes, colours and textures against one another to create a satisfactory idea and a pleasing arrangement.

A bead work design should not only be satisfactory and interesting in both colour, shape and texture, but it must also be suitable and appropriate for the garment, bag etc, for which it is being designed. When designing, bear in mind that the design should fill its allotted space adequately, and the weight of the different parts of the design should be well-balanced. Remember too, that the spaces between the beaded shapes are just as important as the areas of beads. They are all an integral part of the design.

There could be a certain amount of variety in the shapes, but not too many, otherwise the design will be too complex for bead work. The least complicated designs are generally the best for bead embroidery, as a variety of sizes and shapes of beads create the interest. Over-complicated designs will be made even more complex and bitty once the beads are added.

There is much to be considered when designing for bead work. Firstly, try and think of each bead as a single unit in the design, and that the units can be assembled in much the same way as a mosaic. It is this that gives bead embroidery its own special textural and tactile qualities, which raise it above the fabric surface. The qualities of textures play a very important part in modern embroidery, including bead work, and this should always be considered when working out a design. Consider too, when placing the beads against one another whether they should be matt or shiny, large or small, round or even square, and always think of them in relation to the working material. A further point to remember, the fabric is being enriched by an added texture and a surface decoration, thus the whole point of embroidery is to give added interest. Therefore be sure that the beads chosen are really enriching the fabric and not just complicating it. Obviously bear in mind what the design is for and its ultimate use. From this the appropriate materials and beads can be selected.

In the past all types of embroidery, including bead work

tended towards naturalism as this was the fashion. (See figure 3.) At the present time the dominant emphasis is placed on abstract, or non-representational designs, doubtless deriving from contemporary trends in painting and sculpture. These designs are often abstracted from natural objects and are primarily decorative in purpose. They differ from geometric designs which have a long tradition and history and usually contain some symbolism. In fact these were not intended to be entirely decorative though the result may appear so. Bead work lends itself well to geometric designs, for this type of design can be built up quite easily (figure 4). Once the pattern has been laid out, it is just a matter of spacing the beads carefully so that they make a regular geometric pattern. If the shapes are to be solidly beaded, then it is a matter of carefully filling in the shapes with the right colour and size of beads. (Figure 5.)

Apart from abstract or geometric designs, there are also free arrangements where an assortment of colours, shapes and sizes of beads can be played off against one another, building up the design as it goes along. Bear in mind when working in this free way, that the beading should always be in proportion to the shape to which it is being applied. As beads and sequins are often at their best when worked in groups, neither a large all-over linear design, nor a spotted one, are altogether advisable, for the beads look thin and spidery, and tend to get lost in the large expanse of material around them.

There are many different ways of treating beads, as there are beads themselves, and to get the most out of them adopt a bold approach both to the design, the treatment, and the way that they are sewn. Try and be as uninhibited as possible when it comes to working out or trying new ways of attaching them. For instance several beads might be sewn on top of one another, i.e. sequin, bead, sequin, bead, so that they project even further from the surface of the fabric, thus creating a third dimension. (Figure 6.) There are too, many different ways of sewing on a drop bead (see figures 7, 46 and 50) and several layers of beds might also be

3   *Velvet beaded bag, size 152 × 156 mm (6 × 6⅛ in.)
      North American Indian. Author's collection*   ▶

worked over each other. Short strings of beads can be attached to a material, so that they hang in loops, and two bugle beads could also be sewn together so that they stand up as it were on their ends (figure 8).

When several shapes and areas of colour butt up against each other (except in designs of a geometric nature) it is sometimes advisable to mingle some coloured beads from one area with those of another in a different colour, thus blending the shapes more smoothly together. (See colour plate facing page 77.) This will not destroy the shapes, but will make them much more part of the whole design. This could be done with a few simple embroidery stitches, in a colour matching the beads as well as with beads themselves.

It is often thought that beads and sequins should not be over-crowded, in other words they should have a scattered look, or be worked in a repetitive spot arrangement. This is not strictly true, for beads are generally at their best when they are clustered together, so perhaps a rule to remember when designing for bead embroidery is to think of them in groups and massed areas, and treat them boldly. Large areas of beads and sequins are often at their best too, when worked in with a few simple embroidery stitches, such as french knots, bullion knots, chain stitches and couched threads in a lighter or darker tone of the background colour. (See figure 9.) Although beads and sequins work well on their own, the introduction of embroidery stitches helps to build up the flat surface of the fabric to the higher relief of the beads, and sets them off well especially when the stitchery is worked in a variety of threads, silks, cottons and wools which may have either a silky or a matt texture. (See figure 10.)

Naturally beads and machine embroidery can also be used together, but obviously any machine work has to be done before the beads can be applied. (See figure 11.) Remember when combining these two techniques that they should be planned together right from the start. Moreover with hand embroidery, which may be spontaneous and only roughly planned, stitchery may be added at will.

Beads and sequins can be applied to most fabrics, plain or printed (figure 12), smooth or rough, and worked on such surfaces

Text continued on page 35

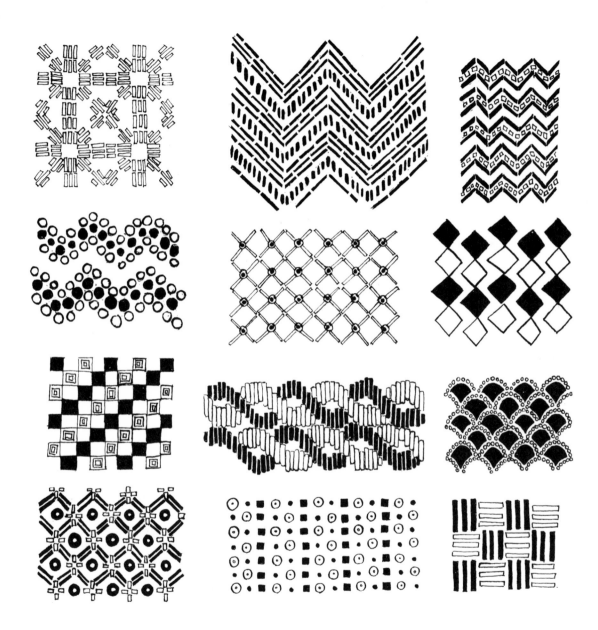

4 *Bead work lends itself well to geometric designs*

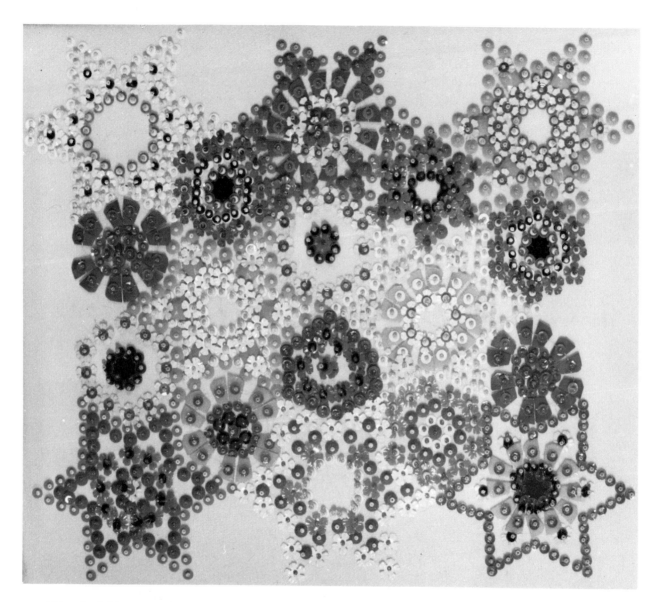

5   *African beaded bag, size 216 × 190 mm (8½ × 7 in.)*
     By courtesy of Constance Howard
6   *Idea worked by Judith Stone, Hornsey College of Art*

7   *Different ways of sewing on a drop bead*

Buttons worked by Lindsey Adams, Eirian Short and Jane Hood; Rosemary Losty and Patricia McLachlan at Wall Hall College; Insung Han at The London College of Furniture, and the author

8   *Evening top. Beads worked round pieces of transparent acetate on a lurex*
    fabric by Jane Simpson, The College of Fashion and Clothing Technology

9 *Detail from chiffon dress, c. 1920, showing couched threads, with glass and chalk beads*
  By courtesy of Constance Howard

10 *Beads and simple stitchery by Pamela Linley, London College of Furniture*

11 *Harem suit, made in silk organza with machine embroidery, Shisha glass, glass beads, plastic mirror, sequins and paillettes by Yvonne Le Rolland, second year Embroidery/Fashion student at Manchester Polytechnic*

12 *Detail showing how a floral print might be treated. Worked by the*
author

13   *Beads worked on a machine-made lace. Worked by the author*

as lace (figure 13), silks, satins, wools and knitted fabrics. In fact nearly all the fabrics that we can buy today can be embroidered with beads, providing the weight of the beaded decoration is consistent with the weight of the material to which it is being applied. Beads and sequins may be used with various embroidery techniques, such as quilting (figure 14), appliqué (figures 15 and 55), smocking, cut-work and canvas work, and may also be strung and made into fringes. Short strings of beads can be couched down onto fabrics too. Beads can be worked in with ribbons as in figure 16, ric rac and braids of all kinds, metal, wool, cotton and silks. Also around raised and padded areas of fabric, leather or pvc as shown in figure 17.

A combination of gold work and beads can also be used most effectively together (see figure 36), and so too can pieces of mica, acetate, large paillettes and beads, which might be of glass, wood or china, or even plastic imitations of all three. Bead embroidery need not only be confined to the surface of a transparent fabric, for instance when two layers of sheer fabric are used together, the first may be richly embroidered with bead work and a second layer could be placed over it. This produces a mysterious quality, by slightly dulling down the beads, and removing their glitter. There is no end to the different combinations of beads and the effects that can be achieved: it is just a matter of being bold and approaching bead work with an open mind when it comes to trying new ways of designing it.

There is an enormous amount of material around us which can be, and has been, used as a basis for design, for example, shells, birds, plants, fish, feathers, pieces of machinery, tools and buildings. (See figures 42, 46, 48, 51, 52 and 53.) Sometimes too advertisements in magazines and newspapers can also be a source of inspiration. Often an idea grows out of a very rough scribble or sketch and it is advisable to keep a notebook in which sketches or jottings can be made. Perhaps 'scrap book' would more correctly describe this book, the object of which is to stimulate the imagination.

When natural or man-made objects fail to inspire designs, then perhaps some quick free methods of working might trigger off a new idea. Start with the materials to see what they will do. For example, when paints are dribbled onto paper and allowed to

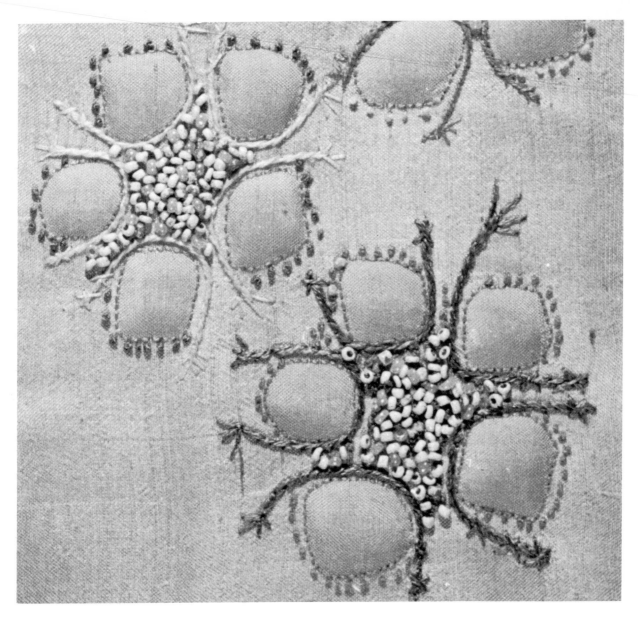

14   *Quilting, stitchery and beads*

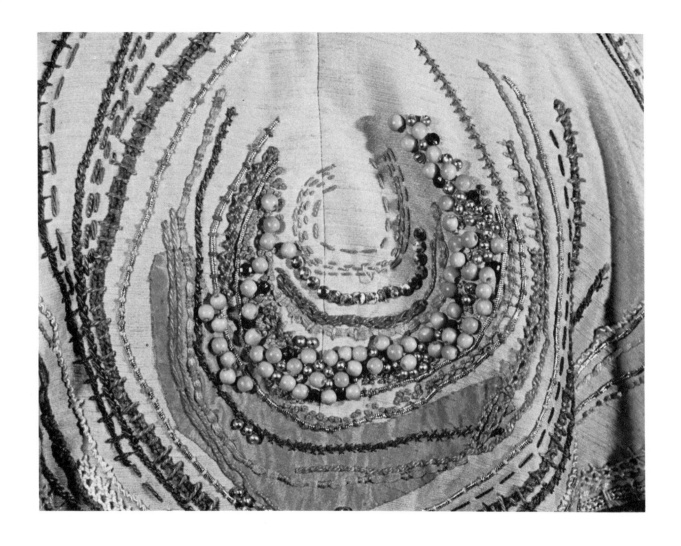

15   *Beads couched threads and silk appliqué*

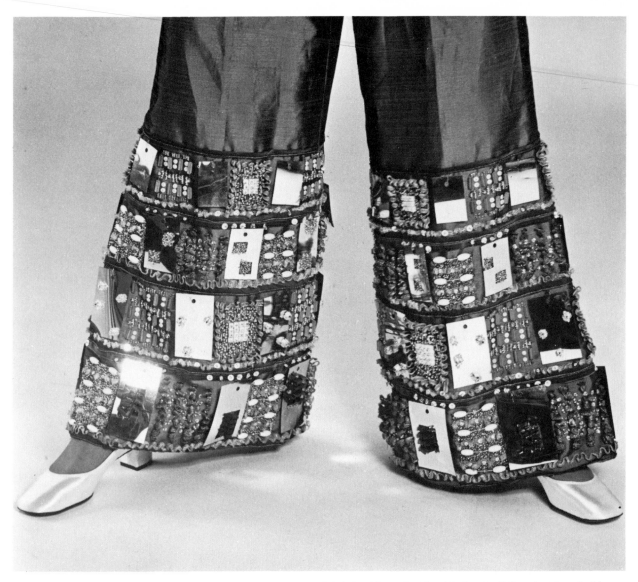

16 *Cat suit. Made in silk, embroidered in bands of silver braids and ribbons, with plastic mirror and a variety of beads by Yvonne Le Rolland, Manchester Polytechnic*

17 *Bag. Bronze kid appliqué, and small round beads worked by Moira Eastern, The College of Fashion and Clothing Technology*

spread freely, they can produce a decorative colour arrangement that could quite easily be freely adapted into bead embroidery. Rubbings from things such as rough wooden floors, or bumpy surfaces, in fact anything with a firm texture (if covered with a thin paper and rubbed with a pencil or wax crayon), will produce patterns that can be translated into bead embroidery. Certain shapes and sizes of dots or small circles are readily interpreted into beads and sequins. This is an asset when the choice of beads and sequins cannot be easily made by the designer, who may be overwhelmed by the wide range of beads available today. Cut and torn paper is another excellent method for working out a design for bead embroidery, for it is not only a free method which helps to clarify the thoughts into some sort of shape, but helps the designer to think and work in massed clusters of beads, rather than in thin lines. Thus bold simple designs are created. These varying approaches to design can often help the inexperienced embroiderer to make a start in bead embroidery, but the individual must be left free to choose her own method of working. Some will always prefer to work out in detail, some will use rough sketches while others will work directly with beads and fabric. This is just a matter of personal choice.

As there are so many varieties of beads, in both gloss and matt, and in contrasting sizes and shapes, there should be little difficulty in working out a satisfactory design, providing there are not too many colours and shapes involved. This great choice in beads means that the design can be built up entirely with the contrasting sizes and shapes of beads – for example, small round ones arranged with long bugles and large paillettes – without the aid of pencil or paper and without a design in mind. Colour can be limited to one, as both shiny and matt beads, or transparent and opaque can be put together in one design, the surface qualities creating the interest instead of the colours (see figure 45).

Before starting on larger pieces of work, it may be advisable to do some experimental samples, using a variety of textures and combinations of beads and sequins and stitchery. Often each new experiment can spark off a fresh idea.

Dress

Dress embroidery is obviously very much bound up with fashion, but fashion changes frequently and sometimes drastically. When beading garments, always bear the current fashion in mind, which may one moment favour the rich and highly elaborate, and the next small and simple motifs.

Bead work should be designed, planned and worked on a garment before it is made up. Ready made garments are not easily embroidered, though separately beaded motifs can be applied to ready-made clothes, but discretion and care will be needed to overcome the various problems that inevitably arise when applying an after-thought to a garment that was initially regarded as complete in itself. The style of the garment must be determined before any bead work can be designed to suit it, as applying beads at random is of little use. If they do not improve the garment, they should be omitted. The purpose of the garment must be clearly defined, be it for formal or informal wear, for day or for evening. It is from this that the appropriate materials can be selected, and the right choice, size, shape, colour of beads can be made.

The many mass produced beaded garments on the market today have a quality that is both mechanical and repetitive, for the designs are governed by the type of machines on which they are beaded. Therefore hand beaded garments should be imaginative, exciting and as rich in texture and colour as they can be if the results are to be more interesting than those produced on a machine. Bead embroidery should both enhance the appearance of a garment, and give it an exclusive look and quality, as well as an *haute couture* finish. All this can be achieved when the embroidery is well designed and worked by hand. When beading on evening wear, wedding dresses or garments designed for special occasions, it is worth bearing in mind that they could have a dramatic and even theatrical appearance, for there is an element of drama attached to these occasions, a point which is frequently overlooked.

Self-coloured embroidery, or that of a lighter or darker tone of the background colour, is probably the most successful way to use beads on day wear (bodice, collar, cuffs, belt, buckles, buttons, on a woollen dress, cardigans, blouse, jumpers, tops, etc). For this it is expedient to use a little hand or machine embroidery in with the beads as this will help to co-ordinate the beads, but can take the evening-wear association away from them. Remember, however to select beads that are not too bright, glittery or shiny. Another important point to bear in mind when beading both clothes and accessories is that the bead work should look well from a distance as well as close to. In the case of dresses, bags and shoes, they are usually first seen from afar, when decoration on them should look good in silhouette as well as being satisfactory at close quarters. To achieve this it is advisable to stop periodically and stand away from the embroidery in order to see it objectively, and before deciding whether or not it is complete. If in any doubt scatter a few beads at random onto the work as this often helps to clarify doubts as well as suggesting new ideas. It is sometimes helpful if each completed piece of a garment is pinned in position onto a dressmaker's dummy and left for a day or so before making the garment up. By doing this a true assessment of the embroidery can be made.

Bead work is a slow form of embroidery involving many hours of work and this point should always be considered when beading an entire dress. If the work is too elaborate and takes a considerable time to complete, the result may be superb but if fashions continue to change as frequently as they have during the last decade then the dress could be out of date by the time it is finished.

Ideally then, with this point in mind it is best to confine bead work to bodices, on both long and short dresses, or down the centre panel of a shirt, midriff or waist band areas. The beads could be thickly massed, gradually thinning out as they work up, down or across the garment. The hems of both long and short dresses could also be treated in this way. When there is some variety in the weight of the pattern this eliminates repetition and monotony, and concentrated areas of beads add richness to the design. Therefore it is advisable to play off beaded areas against plain areas of fabric; this also gives interesting textured effects and helps to keep the garment light as well as preserving its style. Bead embroidery can also be applied to collars, cuffs, yokes and to the inside of a pleat which shows only when the wearer moves.

18 *For day-wear beads which are neither too shiny nor too glittery may be used most successfully. Sketch by Jane Hood*

19 *Sometimes an entire bodice may require beading. Sketch by Jane Hood*

Separately beaded motifs, buttons and small buckles can be used as decoration on soft fabric shoes. The two small buckles shown here are thought to be Edwardian dress trimmings
Buttons and motifs worked by the author

Long and short sleeves also lend themselves to beading and so too do lapels, pockets, buttons, buckles, belts, bags and shoes.

Before embarking on the bead work decide which area or areas are to be beaded and how the interest is to be concentrated in relation to the whole shape, keeping the scheme relatively simple. While working on the embroidery try and capture the mental image of the idea. Remember that the least complicated of designs are generally the most effective, and that they can be destroyed if too many parts of the dress or accessories are embroidered, be it with bead work or stitchery. A richly beaded bodice should not for instance need the addition of a necklace or a brooch, and an embroidered hem of a long dress generally does not benefit by the shoes being similarly beaded, so be discriminating when choosing accessories. It is better to be restrained than to be over-dressed and glittery, thus appearing to have no real understanding of the purpose of clothes. They are intended not only to cover and keep the human form warm, but also to flatter it, to deflect from any imperfections and to give dignity, grace and a sophisticated femine charm to the wearer.

There is a very wide range of both fabrics and colours and when choosing material for a new dress or accessory, take into account the length of time that item is expected to last. If for a long period, then choose a becoming colour, one which is not so assertive that it quickly becomes boring to wear. If the article will have only a short life then the colour may be arresting, but must be suitable for the occasion as well as flattering to the wearer.

A useful hint to consider when choosing colours, is that artificial light generally has a softening effect. The reverse of this is true when colours are subjected to exaggerated lighting, in which some fabrics can be completely drained of both colour and texture. As most fabric departments are lit almost entirely by artificial light there should be no problem when selecting colours for garments that are to be worn in artificially lit environments, but it is advisable to take fabric for day wear out into the daylight so that a true assessment can be made of the colour. One that is beautiful and desirable for evening wear is often quite unsuitable in daylight.

Having selected the pattern for the garment, work out a suitable design, or at least have some idea of how the beads might be treated. Then cut out in paper a duplicate shape of that part of the

20 *This sheet of drawings shows how necklines, cuffs, waist bands, bodices and hem lines might be treated. Sketch by Jane Hood*

21 *Ideas for beading sleeves, lapels and edges of garments.*
    Sketch by Jane Hood

dress pattern that is to be embroidered (if it is to be the bodice, then that is the part to duplicate) and onto this work the design. This becomes a full size working drawing for reference, but does not have to be rigidly copied, in fact the designer may need to add or subtract from the design constantly, for beads do look quite different once they are attached to a foundation material. However, this working drawing will help to keep the beading fresh and lively and prevent the over-working of one area and the neglecting of another. It is advisable to allow for shrinkage when cutting out the garment as thickly massed beads and embroidery have a tendency to draw the fabric up together, thus reducing the overall size of the beaded part of the garment. By doing this the right precautions will have been taken, but if shrinkage does not occur then sew the garment up on the original seam line. As the sewing machine will not of course sew over the beads ensure that the beading ends a little before the seamline. Make up the garment and fill in any gaps in the beading.

It is obviously advisable to make up a toile before embarking on the finished garment. By doing this, not only can alterations to the pattern be easily made, but the design can be worked on to it thus giving an even clearer idea of what the finished garment will be like when complete.

Because fashionable clothes change so frequently, and as there are so many different types of garments – long and short dresses, cloaks, trousers, jumpers, blouses, etc – the best way to cover this wide range of articles is to comment briefly on the various parts of a garment that lend themselves well to bead embroidery.

Remember to allow a little extra material when cutting out a garment, just in case shrinkage takes place and, where possible, line all pieces of bead work as this will prevent the threads getting caught on other articles.

Bodices and yokes

Generally, bodices and yokes of both long and short dresses lend themselves well to bead embroidery. They can be beaded around the neck, across the shoulders as well as down the front towards the waist.

Often an entire bodice may require beading, but take into

account the under arms as thickly beaded areas can catch on sleeves and damage them. Also bare arms can be chafed on over-elaborate bead work.

See figures 19, 22 and 23, also colour plate facing page 60.

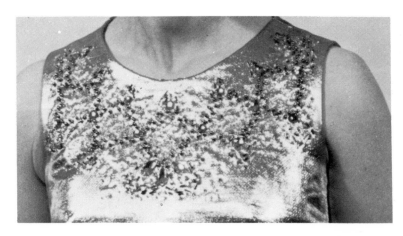

22   *Bodice on gold lamé evening dress by Christine Pittam, Wall Hall College*

23   *Wild silk evening dress. Machine embroidery, sequins and glass beads by a student at Ealing School of Art*

Midriff and waist-band areas

These can be thickly beaded though not necessarily all the way round. If they are cut on the cross grain of the fabric, take care that the weight of the beads does not stretch their shape.
See figures 24 and 25.

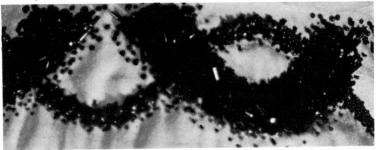

24   Detail from a full length evening dress made from a Dupion fabric by Penny Haigh, Wall Hall College

25   Detail from a full length evening dress with detachable brooch by Lottie Singer, Wall Hall College

Skirts

The hems of both long and short skirts can be beaded most successfully. Hem lines are determined by the prevailing fashion, and on
the type of dress. Whatever length the skirt might be, always be
sure that the hem is an even distance from the ground. Some types
of inverted pleats, or centre panels of skirts can also be beaded.
See drawing figure 20.

Sleeves

There are many different types of sleeves, both long and short,
that lend themselves to bead embroidery. The design should
follow the shape of the sleeves, and not distort them. The beading
can be around the crown, down the sides towards the wrist, and
also down the middle part of a long sleeve. Always embroider
both sleeves at the same time, so that they remain similar, though
a slight difference here and there will be hardly noticed.
See figures 21 and 26, also colour plate facing page 60.

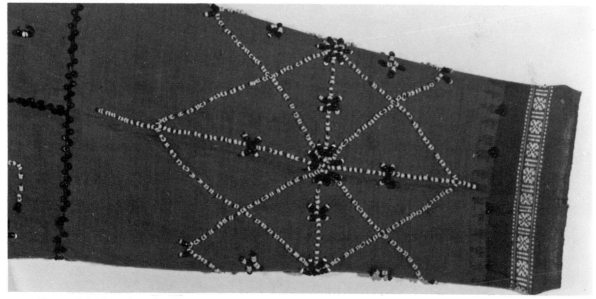

26 *Sleeve of child's jacket of Indian origin*
    By courtesy of Constance Howard

Collars and cuffs

All parts of a garment are important, but collars are a major feature, whatever their size or shape as they frame the face, and should therefore always be made as accurately as possible. Collars with matching cuffs should be designed and worked together for it is easier to work them as a set when they are clearly laid out on a frame.

See figures 27 and 28.

27 *Sequin collar, c. 1920*
By courtesy of Jane Hood

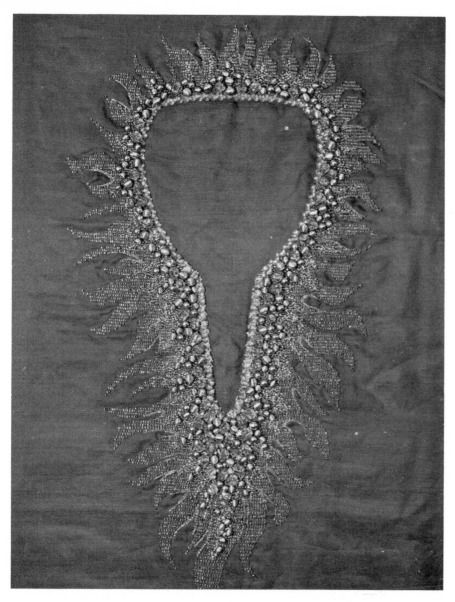

28 *Collar for a kaftan. Worked on chiffon by Noella Watson, The College*
    of Fashion and Clothing Technology

Pockets

Patch pockets and pocket flaps may be beaded, but it is advisable to keep highly beaded pockets purely as a form of decoration. If the pocket is also to be functional ensure when planning that it is wide and deep enough for easy use. The style of the garment will determine the position of the pocket but it should be placed to flatter the figure. Remember too that if the pocket is likely to have regular use, the bead work must be securely sewn.

See figure 29.

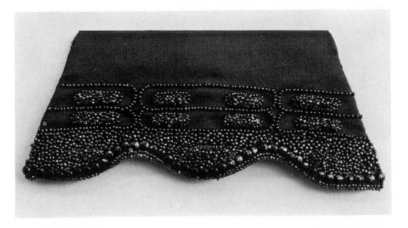

29 *Pocket flap by Ivy Johnson, The College of Fashion and Clothing Technology*

GARMENTS WHICH CAN ALSO BE EMBROIDERED WITH BEADS

Blouses

The once fashionable and feminine frilly blouse has been largely replaced by sweaters, tailored shirts and tops, which are now worn mainly with trousers. However the various parts of an evening blouse – collars, cuffs, sleeves and bodice – can be richly embroidered with bead work.

See figures 30 and 50.

30 *Part of a border for an evening blouse. Silver kid appliqué and crystal beads worked on a green wild silk by Despina Kosti, The College of Fashion and Clothing Technology.* ▶

Knitted jumpers and tops

At the moment knitted jumpers and tops seem to be fashionable for the evening. Like all ready-made clothes, bought jumpers are not easily beaded, and those who knit their own garments are best advised to embroider the various parts before making them up. As most knitted articles are easily stretched it is advisable to space the bead work carefully and keep it evenly weighted.

Cardigans

Up to the present time bead embroidered cardigans have not been considered a necessary part of an English-woman's wardrobe and have not been fashionable in England. Do bear in mind when designing any bead work for this type of garment that it should be evenly distributed.

Boleros and waistcoats

Both types of garment lend themselves particularly well to rich and elaborate bead work as shown by the recent fashion for boleros.

Jackets

The various parts of a loosely fitted or a box type jacket can be beaded most successfully.
See colour plate facing page 60.

Cloaks

Cloaks can be beaded around the hem line, across the shoulders, around the neck, or down the two front panels.

Trousers

The harem styled trousers or those with bell-bottoms lend themselves well to bead work. Do bear in mind though that the edge of a trouser leg will have to take a certain amount of rough treatment, therefore be sure that the beads are securely sewn.
See figure 16.

Accessories

Accessories are important aids to fashion, and should be considered in relation to the garment to be worn.

Belts

These may be part of a dress or sufficiently contrasting and decorative to become an accessory. The shape and width may vary according to the design and to current fashions. Never draw belts up too tightly, as this can spoil the appearance of both the belt and dress. Belts need not be beaded all the way round, but before starting on the embroidery decide on the fastening, for example, with a buckle, with press-stud fastenings, or with hooks and eyes, all of which can be at the front or the back of the belt. In the making of all belts be as neat and as accurate as possible. See figures 31 and 32.

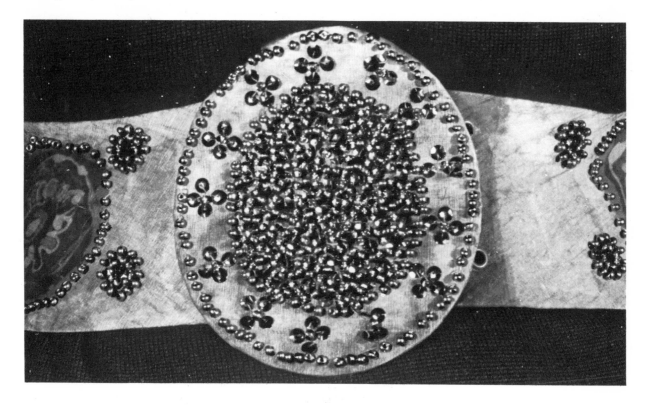

31　*Detail from a batik belt, embroidered with sequins and beads by a student at Ealing School of Art*

Buttons

There are many ways of decorating buttons, some of which render the button unfunctional – however, most beaded buttons are purely decorative.

Beaded buttons can play an important part on a plain dress, and they can be used on coats, cloaks, gloves, cuffs and bags. Each button in a set need not be identical as a slight difference here and there will be barely noticeable and indeed leads to individuality.

See colour plate facing page 28.

Buckles

Remember to design beaded buckles in conjunction with the belt. Apart from being a means of fastening they can also be used decoratively, as on shoes and bags. Button and buckle moulds and shapes can be bought from any good haberdashery department. Be careful not to squash or stretch the bead work when assembling the buckles, which may take a little practice. In cases where buttons or buckles are to be entirely covered in bead work it may be advisable to embroider them after they have been made up.

See figure 33.

33 *Beaded buckles by Lindsey Adams and the author. All these were worked*
on metal shapes bought at a draper's

Hats

Exotic head gear for evening wear, like most things, goes in and out of fashion and until the current craze for wigs of every kind is over hats will remain just trimmings in fashion shows. When beading a hat take into account the outfit with which it is to be worn and choose colours that are flattering to the skin unless it is to be worn as part of a fancy dress outfit.
See figure 1.

Gloves

When gloves neither match the bag nor the shoes, they should match the dress with which they are to be worn. Three-quarter length gloves are generally the most popular, though long ones are best worn with sleeveless full evening dresses. Some ready-made gloves can be beaded but it is important that the tension of the beading thread be kept taut. This is not as easy as may at first appear since each glove in turn has to be stretched over the left hand, thus making it easier to sew on the beads. Once removed from the hand the weight of the beads slackens off the thread. To avoid this, work a small stitch over the back of each bead so that it is firmly held in place.
See figure 34.

Stoles

Stoles can add charm and softness to an outfit, and there are many ways in which they can be worn to give new life to an old dress. One point to bear in mind when beading stoles is to keep both ends evenly weighted, but not too heavily, or they may hang in an uneven fashion.

An evening outfit. Clothes for special occasions can have a dramatic and theatrical quality. The idea which prompted this design was a fantasy Chinese firework display
Designed and worked by the author

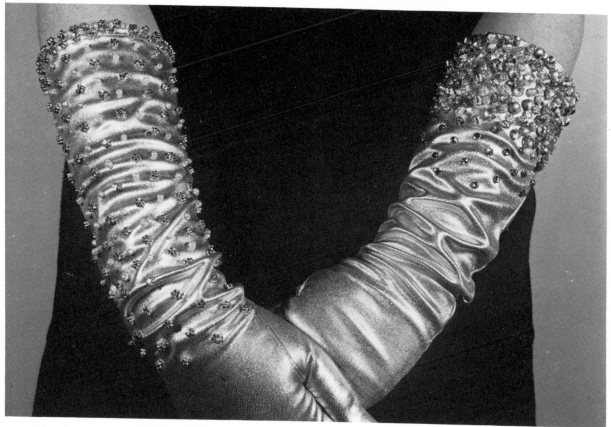

34   *Silver lurex gloves. Worked by the author*

Bags

Virtually any shape or size of bag can be in fashion today, though perhaps small bags are the most attractive and effective. When making a bag that requires stiffening, use either upholsterer's buckram, thin card, or the heaviest quality *vilene*. Nearly all bags will require a lining of some kind and it is advisable to use french seams on these.

See figures 17, 35 and 36.

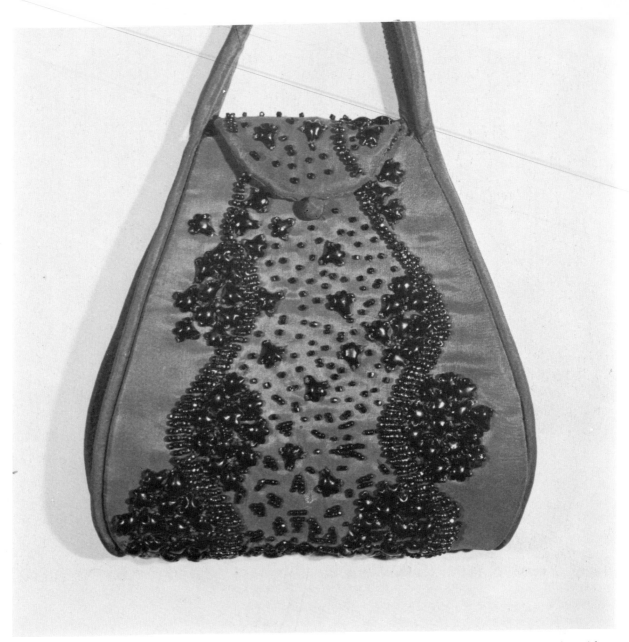

35 *Design for evening bag by Lindsey Adams*

36   *Evening bag. Bugle beads, curtain rings, braids, gold bullion and sequins.*
Worked on a patterned woollen fabric by Kathryn Jackson, third year
Embroidery/Fashion student at Manchester Polytechnic (detail)

Head bands

Because of the growing popularity for hair pieces, head bands are no longer being worn exclusively for day wear. It is possible now to buy ready covered head bands, which can be elaborately beaded and no one should fail to come up with some bright ideas on how to treat the embroidery. Do bear in mind when choosing a head band the garment and the accessories with which it will be worn.

Separately beaded motifs

This type of bead work can be as elaborate as desired and separately beaded motifs can be applied to shoes, bags, stoles, gloves, blouses, dresses and jumpers. They are usually worked on tarlatan, tulle or a fine nylon. Sometimes the back of the motif needs reinforcing with a second layer of fabric, which should be attached with a fabric glue and left to dry. Cut the surplus material away from the embroidery. For attaching beaded motifs use small stitches which should be worked between the bead work.
See colour plate facing page 45.

Shoes

Shoes are made in innumerable styles and colours, which are governed by the latest fashion trend. Separately embroidered motifs, buttons and buckles can be applied to fabric shoes by means of a fabric glue, with staples, or with a few small stitches. Always select shoes that are suitable for the outfit.
See figure 37 and colour plate facing page 45.

Beaded edgings

Beaded edgings are probably the oldest form of bead work. They can still be used with great effect on the edges of garments, such as lapels, cuffs, belts, bags. As edges are inclined to take rather rough treatment during use it would probably be advisable to sew the beads with a double thickness of thread.
See figure 38.

37 *Child's slippers, size 125 mm (5 in.) Leather and velvet, with appliquéd motifs embroidered in glass and chalk beads*
Author's collection

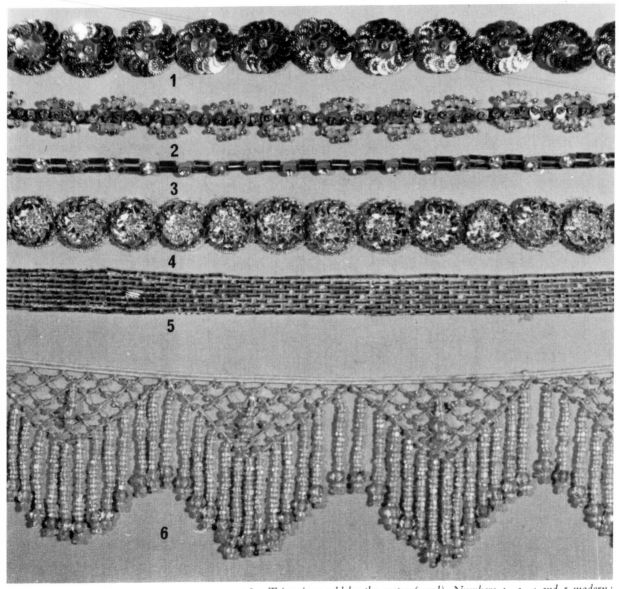

38 *Trimmings sold by the metre (yard). Numbers 1, 3, 4 and 5 modern;*
2 and 6 Victorian
By courtesy of Constance Howard

Beaded fringes

Decorative fringes can be used on stoles, belts, bags and dresses. Bugle beads lend themselves particularly well to this type of bead work.

See figures 38 and 39.

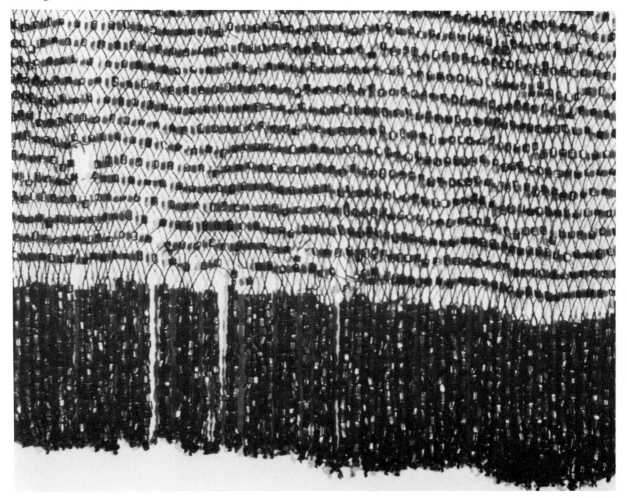

39 *Jet beads strung together giving a chain mail effect*
By courtesy of Constance Howard

Braids and trimmings by the metre (yard)

At the present time a popular form of commercial decoration for garments is that of the elaborately embroidered braids and trimmings which can be bought by the metre (yard). These do have a mechanical, machined quality, but with a little imagination can be improved and made to look more individual and interesting. See figure 38

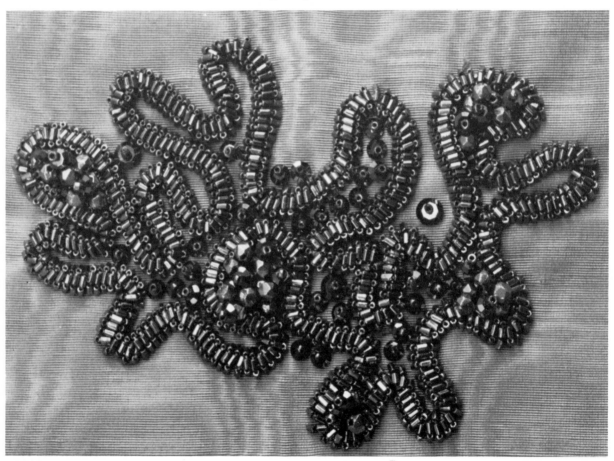

40 *Motif. Bronze beads and sequins worked on a grey moiré silk by Cheuh Wong, The College of Fashion and Clothing Technology*

41 *Detail from a Victorian skirt. Jet beads worked on tulle*
By courtesy of Constance Howard

42   *Ideas may be stimulated by making drawings from plants*

43 *Partly worked design by Judith Stone, Hornsey College of Art. This shows clearly how the design was initially tacked out*

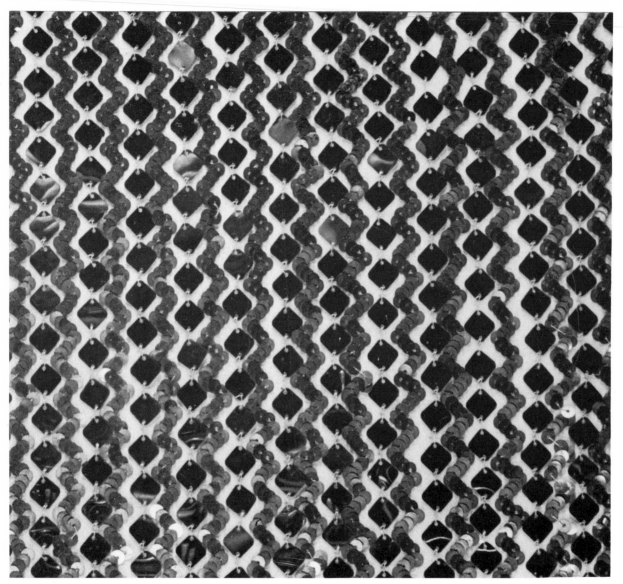

44 *Metal sequins worked on chiffon, c. 1920*
   By courtesy of Constance Howard
45 *Detail. One colour designs can be built up entirely with contrasting sizes*
   and shapes of beads. Worked in silver by the author ▶

74

46 *Design based on fish. Worked in paillettes and sequins by Judith Stone,*
    Hornsey College of Art

47 *Glass beads and sequins on a lace trimming. Worked by the author*
    Overleaf

48 *Detail from sequin dress, c. 1920, with beads and stitchery*
    Author's collection

Circular design. Idea worked by Judith Stone, Hornsey College of Art

49 *Beads, sequins and snake skin by Judith Stone, Hornsey College of Art*

52 *The shapes of feathers and their natural patterns can be a source of inspiration*

53 *Partly worked beading on a screen printed design based on a peacock's feather. Judith Stone, Hornsey College of Art* ▶

54 *Sequins can be used in a variety of ways.*

55 *Silk appliqué, chenille and beads of various sizes. Worked by Barbara Manning, The College of Fashion and Clothing Technology* ▶

84

56 *Motif for a skirt. Silver acetate, sequins, and small bugle beads. Machine appliqué by Madge Robinson. The College of Fashion and Clothing Technology*

57 *Silver neckline decoration on vivid green silk. Worked by Barbara Manning. The College of Fashion and Clothing Technology*

58 *Dress motif on wild silk. Worked by Barbara Manning. The College of Fashion and Clothing Technology*

59 *Gold braid work and gold beads. Worked by Lynn Thompson. The College of Fashion and Clothing Technology*

Suppliers

Most department stores throughout the country sell beads and sequins which usually come in small round boxes.

Firms specialising in beads and sequins

The Bead Shop
South Molton Street, London W1

S. E. Cuming (large quantities only)
64 Margaret Street, London W1

Sesame Ventures
New Invention, Dulverton, Somerset

Amar Pearl and Bead Company Incorporated
19001 Stringway, Long Island City, NY

Hollander Bead and Novelty Corporation
25 West 37th Street, New York 18, NY

Beads, sequins, fabrics and threads

Bourne and Hollingsworth
Oxford Street, London W1

Dickens and Jones
Regent Street, London W1

Ells and Farrier Limited
5 Princes Street, Hanover Square, London W1

D. H. Evans
Oxford Street, London W1

Harrods Limited
Knightsbridge, London SW1

John Lewis
Oxford Street, London W1

The Needlewoman Shop
Regent Street, London W1

Cleaners

Lilliman and Cox Limited
14 Princes Street, Hanover Square, London W1
specialize in beaded garments.

Most well known firms of cleaners will undertake the cleaning of beaded garments but this is done entirely at the owners' risk.